Presidents
of the
United States

LEVEL **3** READER

George Washington
1789–1797

Vice President: John Adams
Political Party: None
State Represented: Virginia
Married: Martha Custis
Lived: 1732 – 1799

General George Washington is called "The Father of His Country." As a general, he helped win the Revolutionary War. His face is on the one-dollar bill. Our Capital city is named after him.

John Adams
1797–1801

VP: Thomas Jefferson
Party: Federalist
State: Massachusetts
Married: Abigail Smith
Lived: 1735 – 1826

John Adams is called "The Father of the Navy." He was the father of the 6th President. He was the first President to live in the White House. He died on July 4—Independence Day!

Thomas Jefferson
1801–1809

VP: Aaron Burr;
George Clinton
Party: Democratic-Republican
State: Virginia
Married: Martha Skelton
Lived: 1743–1826

Thomas Jefferson was an excellent writer and thinker. He wrote most of the Declaration of Independence. He was a governor of Virginia. His face is on the nickel. He died on July 4, the same day as John Adams.

James Madison
1809–1817

VP: George Clinton;
Elbridge Gerry
Party: Democratic-Republican
State: Virginia
Married: Dolley Todd
Lived: 1751–1836

James Madison is called "The Father of the Bill of Rights." He was the shortest President, at 5 feet 4 inches tall. He was a representative from Virginia. His face is on the $5,000 bill—which is no longer used.

James Monroe
1817–1825

VP: Daniel D. Tompkins
Party: Democratic-Republican
State: Virginia
Married: Elizabeth Kortright
Lived: 1758–1831

James Monroe was a governor of Virginia. He implemented the Monroe Doctrine, which said that no other countries could try to colonize the United States. He died on July 4th.

John Quincy Adams
1825–1829

VP: John C. Calhoun
Party: Democratic-Republican
State: Massachusetts
Married: Louisa Johnson
Lived: 1767–1848

John Quincy Adams was the son of the 2nd President. He was the first former President to be photographed, in1848. After his term, he served in Congress for 18 years.

Andrew Jackson
1829–1837

VP: John C. Calhoun;
Martin Van Buren
Party: Democratic
State: Tennessee
Married: Rachel Donelson
Lived: 1767–1845

General Andrew Jackson was called "Old Hickory." He was the very first representative from the state of Tennessee. His face is on the 20-dollar bill.

Martin Van Buren
1837–1841

VP: Richard M. Johnson
Party: Democratic
State: New York
Married: Hannah Hoes
Lived: 1782–1862

Martin Van Buren was a senator and governor from New York. He was the only President who had to learn English later in life. He grew up speaking Dutch.

William Henry Harrison

1841 (March 4–April 4)
VP: John Tyler
Party: Whig
State: Ohio
Married: Anna Symmes
Lived: 1773–1841

General William Harrison was the grandfather of the 23rd President. He was a senator from Ohio. He died in office of pneumonia, and served the shortest time of any President—only one month.

John Tyler
1841–1845

VP: None
Party: Whig
State: Virginia
Married: Letitia Christian (d. 1842); Julia Gardiner
Lived: 1790–1862

John Tyler was a governor and senator from Virginia. He became President after Harrison died. He was the first President to get married in office, and he was the father of 15 children!

11

James Knox Polk
1845–1849
VP: George M. Dallas
Party: Democratic
State: Tennessee
Married: Sarah Childress
Lived: 1795–1849

12

Zachary Taylor
1849–1850 (16 months)
VP: Millard Fillmore
Party: Whig
State: Louisiana
Married: Margaret Smith
Lived: 1784–1850

James Polk was a governor and representative from Tennessee. While he was President, the boundaries of the territories of the United States were stretched to the Pacific Ocean.

General Zachary Taylor was called "Old Rough and Ready." He never voted—until his own election! His horse, Whitey, grazed on the White House lawn. He died after a Fourth of July celebration.

Millard Fillmore
1850–1853

VP: None
Party: Whig
State: New York
Married: Abigail Powers (d. 1853);
Caroline McIntosh
Lived: 1800–1874

Millard Fillmore read the dictionary during breaks as a young mill worker. He was a representative from New York. His wife Abigail started the Presidential Library in the oval room at the White House.

Franklin Pierce
1853–1857

VP: William Rufus De Vane King
Party: Democratic
State: New Hampshire
Married: Jane Appleton
Lived: 1804–1869

General Franklin Pierce was a representative and senator from New Hampshire. When he took office, he was the youngest President up to that time—age 48.

James Buchanan
1857–1861
VP: John C. Breckinridge
Party: Democratic
State: Pennsylvania
Married: Never married
Lived: 1791–1868

James Buchanan was the only President who never married. He was a senator from Pennsylvania. His eyes were unusual: one was near-sighted, the other far-sighted.

Abraham Lincoln
1861–1865
VP: Hannibal Hamlin;
Andrew Johnson
Party: Republican (National Union)
State: Illinois
Married: Mary Todd
Lived: 1809–1865

Abraham Lincoln, "Honest Abe," served during the War Between the States (Civil War) and declared that all slaves were to be free. He was the first President to be assassinated. His face is on the penny and the five-dollar bill. At 6 feet 4 inches tall, he was the tallest President.

Andrew Johnson
1865–1869

VP: None
Party: Democratic (National Union)
State: Tennessee
Married: Eliza McCardle
Lived: 1808–1875

Andrew Johnson was a tailor before he became a senator and governor of Tennessee. While he was President, the United States bought the territory of Alaska from Russia.

Ulysses Simpson Grant
1869–1877

VP: Schuyler Colfax;
Henry Wilson
Party: Republican
State: Ohio
Married: Julia Dent
Lived: 1822–1885

General Ulysses S. Grant was the commander of the United States Army. He changed his name from Hiram Ulysses Grant because he did not want his initials to be H.U.G.

Rutherford Birchard Hayes
1877–1881
VP: William Almon Wheeler
Party: Republican
State: Ohio
Married: Lucy Webb
Lived: 1822–1893

General Rutherford Hayes was a governor from Ohio. He signed a bill that allowed female lawyers to argue cases before the Supreme Court.

James Abram Garfield
1881 (6½ months)
VP: Chester Alan Arthur
Party: Republican
State: Ohio
Married: Lucretia Rudolph
Lived: 1831–1881

General James Garfield was called "The Preacher President." He was a representative from Ohio. He was the first left-handed President. He was the second President to be assassinated.

Chester Alan Arthur
1881–1885

VP: None
Party: Republican
State: New York
Married: Ellen Herndon
Lived: 1829–1886

Chester Arthur became President upon the death of Garfield. During the last years of his term, he was very sick with a kidney disease—but he kept it a secret.

Grover Cleveland
1885–1889

VP: Thomas A. Hendricks
Party: Democratic
State: New York
Married: Frances Folsom
Lived: 1837–1908

Grover Cleveland was a governor of New York. He was the first President to get married in the White House. He is the only President who served terms that were years apart.

23

Benjamin Harrison
1889–1893

VP: Levi P. Morton
Party: Republican
State: Indiana
Married: Caroline Scott (d. 1892);
Mary Dimmick
Lived: 1833–1901

General Benjamin Harrison was the grandson of the 9th President. He was a senator from Indiana. He became President 100 years after the very first President— George Washington.

24

Grover Cleveland
1893–1897

VP: Adlai E. Stevenson
Party: Democratic
State: New York
Married: Frances Folsom
Lived: 1837–1908

Grover Cleveland was also the 22nd President. He was the first President to have a child born in the White House. His face is on the $1,000 bill—which is no longer used.

William McKinley, Jr.
1897–1901

VP: Garret A. Hobart;
Theodore Roosevelt
Party: Republican
State: Ohio
Married: Ida Saxton
Lived: 1843–1901

William McKinley was
a representative and
governor from Ohio. He
was assassinated just six
months into his second
term. His face is on the
$500 bill—which is no
longer used.

Theodore Roosevelt
1901–1909

VP: Charles W. Fairbanks
Party: Republican
State: New York
Married: Alice Lee (d. 1884);
Edith Carow
Lived: 1858–1919

Theodore "Teddy" Roosevelt
was an outdoorsman who
established five National
Parks. When he took office
after McKinley's death, he
was the youngest President,
at 42 years 10 months.
He won the 1906 Nobel
Peace Prize.

William Howard Taft
1909–1913

VP: James S. Sherman
Party: Republican
State: Ohio
Married: Nellie Herron
Lived: 1857–1930

William Taft—"Big Bill"— was the largest President: 6 feet tall, 300 pounds. As President, he started the federal income tax. He served as Chief Justice of the U.S. Supreme Court.

Woodrow Wilson
1913–1921

VP: Thomas R. Marshall
Party: Democratic
State: New Jersey
Married: Ellen Axson (d. 1914); Edith Galt
Lived: 1856–1924

Woodrow Wilson—"The Professor"—was the only President to earn a Ph.D. He served during the Great War (World War I). He signed the 19th Amendment, giving women the right to vote. He won the 1919 Nobel Peace Prize.

Warren Gamaliel Harding
1921–1923

VP: Calvin Coolidge
Party: Republican
State: Ohio
Married: Florence Kling
Lived: 1865–1923

At age 19, Warren Harding ran a newspaper. He was the first President to receive votes from women. In 1922, he was the first President to speak on the radio. He died in office, while traveling back from Alaska.

Calvin Coolidge
1923–1929

VP: Charles G. Dawes
Party: Republican
State: Massachusetts
Married: Grace Goodhue
Lived: 1872–1933

Calvin Coolidge was born on July 4! He was a governor of Massachusetts. He took office upon the death of Harding, and was sworn in by a justice of the peace in Vermont—who happened to be his own father.

Herbert Clark Hoover
1929–1933

VP: Charles Curtis
Party: Republican
State: California
Married: Lou Henry
Lived: 1874–1964

Herbert Hoover was an adventurer and became a multi-millionaire by age 40. He was President at the start of the Great Depression. After his presidency, he was chairman of the Boys' Clubs of America for eight years.

Franklin Delano Roosevelt
1933–1945

VP: John N. Garner; Henry A. Wallace; Harry S. Truman
Party: Democratic
State: New York
Married: Eleanor Roosevelt
Lived: 1882–1945

Franklin Roosevelt was a 5th cousin of the 26th President. He suffered from polio at age 39, and never walked unaided again. He was President during World War II. He was elected four times and served longer than any President— 12 years 1 month. His face is on the dime.

Harry S. Truman
1945–1953

VP: Alben W. Barkley
Party: Democratic
State: Missouri
Married: Bess Wallace
Lived: 1884–1972

Harry Truman had no middle name—he added the "S." He was a senator from Missouri. A sign on his desk read "The Buck Stops Here." He served during the end of World War II.

Dwight David Eisenhower
1953–1961

VP: Richard M. Nixon
Party: Republican
State: Pennsylvania
Married: Mamie Doud
Lived: 1890–1969

General Dwight Eisenhower, nicknamed "Ike," was Commander of Allied Forces in Europe during World War II. He was the first President to serve after the 50th state was added to the union.

35

36

John Fitzgerald Kennedy
1961–1963

VP: Lyndon B. Johnson
Party: Democratic
State: Massachusetts
Married: Jacqueline Bouvier
Lived: 1917–1963

John Kennedy—"J.F.K."—was the first Catholic President, the first to be born after 1900, and the youngest to be **elected**. His book, *Profiles in Courage*, won the Pulitzer Prize. He was assassinated in Dallas. His face is on the 50-cent coin.

Lyndon Baines Johnson
1963–1969

VP: None; Hubert H. Humphrey
Party: Democratic
State: Texas
Married: Claudia "Lady Bird" Taylor
Lived: 1908–1973

Lyndon Johnson—"L.B.J."—was a teacher, a rancher, and a senator from Texas. He took the oath of office while aboard the presidential jet, *Air Force One*, upon the death of Kennedy.

Richard Milhous Nixon
1969–1974

VP: Spiro T. Agnew;
Gerald R. Ford
Party: Republican
State: California
Married: Thelma "Pat" Ryan
Lived: 1913–1994

Richard Nixon was a senator from California. He was President when the first man walked on the moon. He was accused of being involved in an illegal cover-up, and was the first President to resign from office.

Gerald Rudolph Ford, Jr.
1974–1977

VP: Nelson A. Rockefeller
Party: Republican
State: Michigan
Married: Elizabeth "Betty" Bloom
Lived: 1913–2006

Gerald Ford turned down a contract with the National Football League. He was a representative from Michigan for 25 years. He was appointed Vice President, and then became President when Nixon resigned—so he was never actually elected into office.

James "Jimmy" Earl Carter, Jr.
1977–1981
VP: Walter Mondale
Party: Democratic
State: Georgia
Married: Rosalynn Smith
Lived: 1924–Present

Ronald Wilson Reagan
1981–1989
VP: George H.W. Bush
Party: Republican
State: California
Married: Jane Wyman;
Nancy Davis
Lived: 1911–2004

Jimmy Carter was called "The Peanut President" because his family had run a peanut farm. He was a governor of Georgia. After his term, he won the 2002 Nobel Peace Prize.

Ronald Reagan was an actor, who appeared in 53 films, and a governor of Califonia. He was wounded in an assassination attempt, and joked, "I forgot to duck." He was the oldest President: 69 years 11 months to 77 years 11 months.

George Herbert Walker Bush
1989–1993
VP: Dan Quayle
Party: Republican
State: Texas
Married: Barbara Pierce
Lived: 1924–Present

George H.W. Bush was U.S. Ambassador to the United Nations and Director of the CIA. He was President during the Persian Gulf War. He is the father of the 43rd President.

William Jefferson Clinton
1993–2001
VP: Albert Gore, Jr.
Party: Democratic
State: Arkansas
Married: Hillary Rodham
Lived: 1946–Present

William "Bill" Clinton was a saxophone player and had thought about becoming a musician. He was governor of Arkansas at age 32. He was President during the launch of the first White House website.

George Walker Bush
2001–2009
VP: Richard Bruce Cheney
Party: Republican
State: Texas
Married: Laura Welch
Lived: 1946–Present

Barack Hussein Obama II
2009–Present
VP: Joseph R. Biden, Jr.
Party: Democratic
State: Illinois
Married: Michelle Robinson
Lived: 1961–Present

George W. Bush is the son of the 41st President. He was a manager of the Texas Rangers baseball team and a governor of Texas. He was President during the terrorist attacks of September 11, 2001, and the war in Iraq.

Barack Obama is the first African-American President. His father was from Kenya, and his mother was from Kansas. He was a senator from Illinois. He is one of the youngest Presidents, taking office at age 47.

Prez Quiz!

1) Who was the youngest person to hold the office of President?

2) Who was the youngest person to be *elected* President?

3) Who was the oldest President? The shortest?
The tallest? The biggest?

4) Who was the first President to live in the White House?

5) Who was the first President to have a child born
in the White House?

6) Which Presidents died on July 4?

7) Which President was born on July 4?

8) Which Presidents had sons who became President?

9) Which Presidents won the Nobel Peace Prize?

ANSWERS: 1) Theodore Roosevelt; 2) John F. Kennedy; 3) Ronald Reagan, James Madison, Abraham Lincoln, William Taft; 4) John Adams; 5) Grover Cleveland; 6) Thomas Jefferson, James Monroe; 7) Calvin Coolidge; 8) John Adams (John Quincy Adams), George H.W. Bush (George W. Bush); 9) Theodore Roosevelt, Woodrow Wilson, Jimmy Carter